CW01376168

DANDELION DAYS

A LIFE IN PROSE AND POETRY

DANDELION DAYS

A Life in Prose and Poetry

BY

PAM NOYES

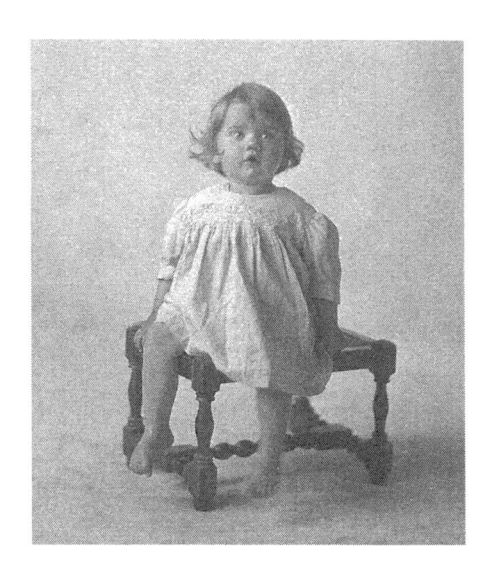

THE BREWSTER PRESS
STANHOE, KING'S LYNN, NORFOLK
2013

Published 2013 by The Brewster Press
Stanhoe, King's Lynn, Norfolk PE31 8QD
Tel: (01485) 518 232
www.thebrewsterpress.com
email: info@thebrewsterpress.com

Typeset in Sylfaen 10 point

Copyright © Pam Noyes 2013

Dandelion Drawings
Copyright © Auriel Mims 2013

Cuckoo Drawing
Copyright © Pam Noyes 1982

Printed and bound in the UK
by the MPG Books Group,
Bodmin and King's Lynn

ISBN 978-0-9572790-1-8

Every effort has been made to contact all copyright holders, but if any have been inadvertently overlooked, the publisher will be pleased to make the necessary arrangements before the next reprint.

For Murray,

Susie and Gary,

*Saffi, Matthew, Tammy,
James, Luke, Edward, Joshua, and Sam*

*and
Bradley, Olivia, Dylan*

ACKNOWLEDGEMENTS

My thanks to everyone who has urged me to write, but in particular to Anabel Symington for her encouragement and criticism, to Caroline Gilfillan for her excellent tuition, to the editors of *Between the Land and the Sea* for the inclusion of one of my poems, and to my dear husband, Murray, who has played such a big part in my life.

I would like, too, to thank Auriel Mims for her suggestions and her drawings of the dandelions that divide up the book.

Also my grateful thanks to Michael Bell, my exacting editor and publisher at The Brewster Press, for his sound advice and painstaking attention to detail.

The Editor wishes to thank Mr Raymond Monbiot for additional information used in the introduction.

Tide Turn was published in the Burnham Market Community Anthology *Between the Land and the Sea* in July 2012.

*To me the meanest flower that
blows can give thoughts that do
often lie too deep for tears.*

William Wordsworth

CONTENTS

Introduction					5

Home						9
Father						11
Mother						14
Sugar Lips					16
Sunday School				17
Blue and White Summer		18
Drawers						20
Candle Sweets				24
Village Kids				25
Tea Party					26
The Hall Chair				27
Evacuation					28
Words-worth					30
On the Beach				31
Soft White Sliced			32
Draughts					34

Lady in Green	37
Piggy	38
Elly	39
Stream	40
November Garden	41
Whiteout	42
November Walk	44
Windy Shore	45
The Sea	46
Tide Turn	47
Eggshells	48
Rounded	49
Sweet Peas	50
Blabbery	51
Next Time, Biro	52
Sharp Fins	53
Greedy Pig	54
Hurray	55
Cow	56
Snowdrops	58
Recycling	59
Fiona	60
Blood	62
September Walk	63
On Finding a Girl's Body in a Wood	64

Emergence	67
The Stream	68
A Grandmother's Story	70
The Lane	71
My Sailor	72
Night Sail	73
Zimmer Frame	74
Old Sailor	75
Unravelling	76
Frozen	77
Mirror Image	78
Insomnia	79
Diamond	80
May	81
Shutterings	82
Unknowing	84
Windows of Summer	85
Rose	86
Days	87
Christmas	88
What are we?	89
Time Bomb	90
Cuckoo	92
My Bloke	93
Baby Sitting	94
The Dance	95
Portrait	96
November Chorus	97
Saffron Moon	98

INTRODUCTION

As one of four daughters of a stern man of the cloth born at the height of Queen Victoria's reign, Pam Noyes endured a relatively strict upbringing in rural Norfolk where her father was a country parson. With a social position to maintain, a wife twenty years his junior, a conspiracy of unruly offspring and an extensive parish to run, he had his hands full. The stories Pam recounts of her early days provide a flavour of a child's view of life during the years leading up to the second world war under the benevolently autocratic rule of a loving father.

She was born in 1929 in the large medieval rectory at Elsing which her father had taken three years earlier as his first living after ordination. The house was said to have been haunted, a fact corroborated to the consternation of the children by her psychic grandmother who claimed to have encountered a 'grey lady' walking along the landing accompanied by the audible rustling of her long skirts.

When she was six, however, her father was translated to the joint benefice of Saxlingham and Field Dalling and the family moved into the beautiful Georgian rectory at Saxlingham with its five acres of grounds including woodlands, a tennis court and the stables where they eventually kept their ponies and goats and which was to be the scene of most of the stories recounted in the first part of this book. Her father remained there as Rector until his death twenty-six years later from heart failure at the age of 79. Her mother outlived him until her own death nine years later at the age of 63 in 1970.

Pam is known throughout Norfolk as a painter, but in this volume we discover a different side to her, that of writer and poet. The body of work as a whole is arranged in chronological order of relevance and falls interestingly into predominantly prose at the start and then, as she progresses through her life, increasingly into the poetry through which she expresses her feelings towards events. The style is down to earth and inquisitive.

Much towards the end is taken up with the manner in which she copes with the increasing debility of Murray Noyes, the great love of her life and her husband of 64 years whom she married at the age of nineteen after meeting him on the beach at Burnham Overy Staithe. Old age is also a major theme — as, too, is the silence of nature.

Everyone who reads this will find something that strikes a chord.

Editor

HOME

My childhood was spent in a huge, cold rectory in Norfolk with my parents, my three sisters and my brother. Only in summer did we feel warm. Winters were a nightmare of huddling round a temperamental fire in what we called the Breakfast Room. The big rooms were closed off until Easter, unless the bishop or some other dignitary came to tea. Ella, our living-in maid, would then be asked to light the fire in the drawing room; but as the room was so vast, it made little difference and a cold mist seemed to hang suspended in mid-air.

I was constantly plagued by chilblains on my fingers and toes, great purple itching lumps that bled when I scratched them – which I did nearly all the time. Hot-ache was another thing: after snowballing or some other activity that made my hands go numb with cold, I would thrust them half way up the chimney to warm them. But the agony that ensued was scarcely bearable. "Ow, ow, ow" I danced around, shaking my hands.

"Whatever is the matter with you?" my mother asked me one day from her armchair pulled up as close to the fire as she dared, a small plaid rug draped over her legs to prevent them from becoming mottled from the heat. Looking up from her Barbara Cartland she reached for a Park Drive, lit it and, inhaling the smoke, said "Sit down, Darling, you're making me nervous."

We did everything in this room. There was a large table in the middle draped by a green chenille covering with little tassels hanging off it. At meal times a linen cloth was spread over it and Ella waited on us at table serving unappetising meals of boiled rabbit and potatoes, or runny shepherd's pie that my mother had made in the scullery as she battled with the paraffin stove whose fumes pervaded the house. Unfortunately my mother was not a natural in the kitchen, and we were obliged to eat whatever she produced. On Saturdays we had a roast, not Sundays – as was the tradition in most homes – because Sunday was my father's working day.

MY FATHER

My father was over 40 when I was born. So I never knew him as a young man. He never talked about his childhood in Cornwall or about his parents or siblings.

He was a mystery person, keeping to his study, writing out his sermons for Sunday, doing football pools and backing horses on the phone. He was tall with brown hair which always smelled of bay rum and he had vivid blue eyes. My mother used to tell us it was those eyes she fell for – as well as his voice – when, fresh out of convent, she became his secretary at 18. Of course all the village women in the bat-infested pews on Sunday mornings were mesmerized by his deeply modulated voice as they gazed up at him in the pulpit expounding the Word Of God, his white surplice and collar accentuating his tanned face.

His countenance at all times was one of authority. He was a product of the late Victorian era of snobbery, eccentricity, knowledge and education. At 23 he was an MA; he then became an army captain in India, trained for the Church and was ordained in 1924. In 1926 he married my mother and proceeded to fill the rectory with five children – with me in the middle.

My father always smelled of tobacco as well as the lotion he put on his hair. When he died I took one of his tweed jackets home and hung it in my hall. I got into the habit of burying my face in the rough cloth, trying to conjure up the feeling that he was somehow still with me. But after a few years the smell faded and it was just a coat. I miss him to this day, even after more than 50 years. Although the coat has long since fallen off the hook, if I close my eyes I can see him still and smell his wonderful rich aroma. And I know I shall never meet anyone like him again.

My father was a mixture of good humour, bad temper and snobbery and we never knew which of these characteristics would emerge at any given time or circumstance. Sometimes he would laugh at something and at others the same thing would infuriate him. So life with him was a kaleidoscope of differing moods as the family swayed back and forth on the tides of his emotions.

He had a sense of humour that burst out of him, sometimes at extremely inopportune moments. The Rural Dean and his wife came to tea one afternoon and were welcomed by our miniature pony Dinah entering the drawing room and depositing a smelly present for them on the carpet, causing my father to rise to close the curtains in an attempt to stifle the laughter he could not control.

He was also a compulsive auction-goer and we never knew what he would be buying or selling next. Furniture vans crept up and down the drive with heaven-knows-what inside, bringing stuff in and taking stuff out. As a result, we would one day be sitting round a Queen Anne table and the next be back to scrubbed pine. He once bought a set of beautiful beds with feather mattresses which we adored, but they, too, were sold on and we returned to our iron bedsteads with their lumpy mattresses through which we could feel the springs.

On one occasion he announced he had bought a school in a coastal village: a convent complete with nuns, pupils and staff. It was up and running and simply changed hands. He said he had bought it for his four daughters and one son in case they ever took up teaching. He did that kind of thing and I think, from what my mother told me at the time, he must have had a substantial win on the pools because in those days a parson's stipend was certainly not enough to buy schools overnight.

MY MOTHER

My mother was a restless soul, a caged bird, beautiful and wild, her wings clipped by her status as a parson's wife and the expectation of my father that she should be an asset to him in the parish. But as time went on and five children later, she became increasingly bored with the eternal church services, the cleaning of the altar brasses and stuffy meetings in the dank village hall among the grey felt hats and sensible shoes of the moustached ladies of the parish.

Everyone loved my mother. She was soft and pliable, generous to the core, giving and easy-going and fun to be with. She always smellled of cigarette smoke and Pond's *Cold Cream*. Her hair was light brown and permed into a soft halo around her sweet face, her large dove-grey eyes looking out on the world with naivety and expectation. Men of all shapes and sizes and from all walks of life were strangely attracted to her. She seemed to exude an extraordinarily unselfconscious invitation to all and sundry. In fact she did have an affair with a local landowner once, a brief encounter that ended abruptly when my father found out.

My mother hated protocol, rebelling against the 'do-gooders' and 'stuffed shirts'. She loved spontaneous conversation and the presence of what she called 'real' people. She was highly creative and spent hours on the nearby beaches collecting cockle shells and turning them into little figures for children and painting them with bright colours.

She loved make-up, clothes and 'going out' — a party girl thwarted by circumstances, with now and again a little bit of her trickling through, delighting us all and relaxing the sometimes austere atmosphere of the rectory.

She just seemed to go with the flow in her own sweet way. In fact I don't remember her ever showing any emotion at all. And, provided she had her cigarettes and her glass of sherry, with the odd flirtation thrown in, she was happy.

My father, however, was extremely jealous and he watched my mother like a hawk.

"Where are you going?" he demanded whenever he saw her getting out her bike.

"Oh, just to the shop in Field Dalling to get some cigarettes," she would answer. And he would mutter and grumble until she returned pink-faced and bright-eyed.

Of course *we* all knew that she had been to see *HIM*, a local farmer with whom she was currently having a flirtation ...

SUGAR-LIPS

One day, after we had all sat down to the dreaded rabbit stew, my father and mother seated one at each end of the table and we four girls on either side, Ella – who had rather full lips anyway – looked a bit different as she was serving the meal. We sniggered and wriggled and wondered if Father would notice. Before lunch we had dared Ella to serve at table wearing the huge pair of red sugar-lips she had bought in a sweet shop on her day off and which could be kept in place by biting on the middle bit that stuck into your mouth. We couldn't contain ourselves and tears ran down our cheeks as we tried to smother our laughter.

"Ella," he roared, "go and wipe that muck off your mouth."

"Oh I'm sorry, Sir", said Ella in a muffled voice.

"Why can't you speak?" demanded my father.

And with that Ella removed the enormous pair of sweet-lips, letting a long trail of saliva dribble down her front.

"Oh my god," shrieked my mother, eliciting a stern look from my father.

We never saw what happened next. For by this time we had left the table, bent double in an explosion of pent-up laughter as we ran through the kitchen door and out into the yard, scattering the squawking hens.

SUNDAY SCHOOL

Sunday was my father's working day when we all had to troop across the road to the little Norman church over which he presided and where my mother held a Sunday-school in the afternoon.

My sisters and I were there among the village kids with their runny noses. One Sunday when I was five, I was desperate to have a pee. We were all sitting on a long bench in the small side room with my mother on a chair reading bible stories to us. I was seated at the end of the bench and, unfortunately for the other children, my end was slightly higher than theirs and ... I wet my knickers.

The ensuing flow of pee, once it got going, seeped down the row of bottoms sitting on the bench and, one by one, they moved to the other end, shuffling and glaring at me until they all landed in a heap on the floor. "Pam! Go home and change your knickers", my mother muttered in my ear.

"Well, I think we'll finish for today," she announced. "You can all go home now". And with "Cor, look at my trousers" and "my dress is all wet", their voices faded as they went out of the door to heaven-knows-what from their mothers. Most had only a well in the garden from which to draw their water which they did by turning a squeaking iron handle with a bucket on the end of a rope. To make matters worse, they were wearing their Sunday best.

For weeks after that I didn't play in the village.

BLUE AND WHITE SUMMER

Our school uniform was mainly grey – skirt, coat, hat and socks – except for a sky-blue jumper and a blue band around the hat with the words "Start Point". Start Point was a private girls' school attended by around thirty pupils.

In summer we wore blue and white floral dresses. Our mothers were issued with lengths of material either to make them up themselves or to engage a professional dressmaker. My mother, always frugal, tried to make mine herself, the result being a disaster that caused many a titter among my peers – uneven hems, badly set collars, enormous puffed sleeves and sloping shoulders. I hated them and longed for the summer to be over, so I would no longer have to compete with the girls from the more affluent families who strutted about in their beautifully cut, professionally finished dresses with button-holes that actually met the buttons on the front.

My mother got carried away, imagining for herself a new career as a fashion designer, and went berserk creating matching knickers which turned out to be huge bloomers that hung down my legs because the elastic was too loose. I found myself constantly hitching them up under my armpits.

I mercifully outgrew them fast and, by the following year, she had developed an interest in making gnomes out of seashells – handing the blue and white lengths of cotton to a local seamstress.

DRAWERS

"I'm going to the auction at the Feathers", my father announced one Saturday morning as we were finishing breakfast. "Anyone want to come?"

"I'll go," I said.

I loved the auctions with my father. His Cornish blood led him into all sorts of tinkeries, one of which was wheeling and dealing. Furniture, ponies, donkeys and goats changed hands with alarming speed throughout my childhood and from one month to the next, my sisters and I never knew what bed we would be sleeping in, nor what table we would be sitting at. There seemed to be a constant rumbling of removal vans and farmers' carts coming and going along our drive.

I stood beside him in my outgrown coat and hand-me-down shoes, shivering as the lots came and went in the huge draughty outbuilding that was generally used for cattle and sheep sales. We sometimes came to these as well, where once my father bought eleven goats – four British Alpine, two Nubian and five beautiful white Saanen. It fell to us of course to look after them, milking them before we went to school, and again in the evening. This motley herd stayed with us for about two years until Father decided one day that he had had enough: they were always getting out of their pen and eating the roses and anything else in sight, including the washing on the line. So he sold the lot to a local farmer at one of the livestock sales where khaki-coated men with cigarettes hanging off their lips and sticks in their hands, drove the cattle round while red-necked farmers in tweed jackets and flat caps nodded their bids to the gabbling auctioneer. "How on earth does anyone understand what he is saying?" I wondered, fascinated by the relentless torrent of sound gushing from his mouth.

This day a big house sale was taking place and a large quantity of fine furniture was being sold. My father had been rummaging about before the sale and said to me "Look at this, Pam," running his hand over an enormous chest of drawers, "maple, and there's a whole lot of it." I looked around and saw at least ten or twelve enormous pieces of bedroom furniture. Of course when it came up he bought the lot, nodding his bids against the others. "£200 pounds," the auctioneer babbled, "going, Going, GONE! to the Reverend." And the hammer fell.

Once Father had arranged for the furniture to be delivered, we went through to the saloon bar of the Feathers Hotel and had sandwiches with beer for him and lemonade for me, warming our hands by the inglenook fire. Father was very pleased, as always when he thought he'd got a bargain. "It will all look splendid at home, Pam. You and Gorly can have one of the beds if you like." That, I thought, would certainly be an improvement on the camp beds we were used to sleeping on with their thin, lumpy mattresses.

The furniture was delivered the following day and that night Gorly and I climbed into the most luxurious bed we had ever slept in, complete with feather mattress and pillows.

I must have been nine years old and Gorly seven.

The rest of the beautiful pieces were spread about in the other bedrooms, each of my sisters having a comfortable bed and a chest of drawers of their own and my mother the dressing table with its oval mirror.

So for a time our 'upstairs' was rather grand, until the day Father heard of a large country house sale soon to be held near Norwich. "I wonder what that maple set would fetch there," he mused to my mother, and with that he was on the phone, booking the furniture into the sale which was to take place in two weeks.

But before that the four of us had an idea.

It was the school holidays and we were always on the look-out for something to do. The water meadows behind the church were flooded and we wanted to go boating and were trying to think what we could use as a boat. Suddenly Ann piped up "What about that biggest drawer in the chest in my bedroom?"

"Oh yes," cried Pat and started hopping about in glee. And with that we were off, tearing across to the rectory and up the stairs into Ann's bedroom. We tipped out the clothes and lugged the heavy drawer down the stairs, out of the house, past the church and into the water-meadow.

Father was at a meeting, so we knew he'd be away for the afternoon.

The drawer actually floated and, getting into it two at a time, we paddled with bits of wood up and down the swamp. It was the most wonderful adventure. Some of the village kids came to have a go as well when they heard all the shrieks from the meadows.

Reluctantly we had to leave the meadows when we thought our father was due to come home. So we carried our boat back and, after drying it with a towel in the bedroom, tried to push it back into its place ... but it wouldn't go in! It had swollen in the water.

So we had to leave it to dry, hoping desperately that no one would come into the bedroom before it had shrunk enough to fit. Next morning, after a lot of pushing, it went in ... but only just.

And to this day I wonder if the people who bought the suite at the country house sale ever managed to pull that drawer open again.

CANDLE SWEETS

I remember a candle flickering in my bedroom when I was very young. When a small draft passed the yellow flame, it moved and swayed. I used to watch it until I fell asleep. Sometimes I stayed awake as the white column got shorter and lumpier – with the melting wax clinging to the sides and forming a magic castle of towers and turrets. The candle stood in a blue enamel candlestick shaped like a large saucer with a handle at the side.

Every morning, the first thing I did was to put my hand out into the saucer to see if He had left them: every night on his way to bed, my Father would come to my room and to my sisters' rooms and place two sweets in each candlestick.

This went on until the war when sweets were rationed and our morning treat faded away like the yellow flame that had comforted me during the scary nights of my childhood.

VILLAGE KIDS

1938

"I've told you not to go into the village. You've got five acres of grounds here. I've bought you ponies, goats and rabbits. Why do you have to go and mix with these dreadful cottage-dwellers? I am the vicar here and I expect you to set a good example."

My father, red-faced and furious, had caught us up the road in a hay-barn jumping off wagons and rolling about among the bales.

Although my three sisters and I loved looking after our animals, we had a great desire to explore and find out how the 'village people' lived, and we were fascinated by the tiny rooms of cottages that housed perhaps a family of seven or eight, all living in a two-up-two-down and a privy up the garden with squares of newspaper on a string hanging on a nail.

"Get home, you Heathen. How dare you disobey me."

The kids we were playing with scuttled like rats out of the big barn doors. We, on the other hand, were driven back home along the road like sheep, Father wielding a stick he had pulled out of the hedge and whacking the road in fury – not *us*, I'm glad to say, though it came perilously close once or twice as I felt the swish on the back of my cotton dress.

TEA PARTY
1941

The Diocesan Bishop and his wife were on their annual visit to our house and my mother had prepared tea in the drawing room. She had made rock cakes that more than lived up to their name, and had got out the best china.

My two older sisters and I had been instructed to appear briefly during the visit, dressed in our school uniforms which were the only decent clothes we had.

We sat bored and fidgeting as the Bishop and Father droned on about Parish affairs, until the unexpected happened. The Bishop's wife caught her elbow on the wing of the armchair, spilling her tea all over a cushion. Trying to mop it up with her handkerchief, she extracted a magazine from the depths of the chair. "Oh dear" she said, "I hope this has not been spoilt". As she held it up we froze: it was one of Ella, the maid's, Penny Dreadfuls that my mother must have been secretly reading the evening before, hurriedly stuffing it behind a cushion on hearing the approaching steps of my father who would have been furious had he caught her reading such 'filthy trash'.

My mother took the offending magazine from the Bishops wife's hand as gently as possible, but not before the whole company had seen the front cover which depicted a half-naked lady with a man bending lecherously over her. Secreting it discretely between some books on a side table she said "I really must have a word with that girl" and, turning a little pink, poured the Bishop's wife another cup of tea.

THE HALL CHAIR

There was a carved oak chair placed in the wide hall of my school where we were banished to sit if the headmistress considered we should be punished. This was

THE DREADED HALL CHAIR

round which we sidled *en route* for different classrooms or the dining area.

One day after lunch, I went to the lavatory during reading time. I took my book with me and forgot to bring it back. Mrs Crumb, the headmistress, asked me where my book was and I said "I left it in the lavatory". To my surprise she told me "Go and sit on the Hall Chair".

Whether she'd had a row with her husband or was just in a bad mood, I'll never know. But off I had to go and endure the sniggers and stares of my classmates as they filed past me on their way to afternoon lessons.

I have never forgotten it because, to this day, I still have no idea what on earth I had done wrong.

EVACUATION
- 1940 -

Come out, come out from the dark spill of the night.
Ink on my blotting paper, the smell of boys unwashed,
hateful and terrifying motes of dust in the squares
of sunlight that fall across ink-stained desks and nit-ridden heads.

I feel sick.
I want to go home.
Home?
It's not my home. It's my aunt's house
Where we are squashed into one room, quarrelling and evacuated.

"Get away from the bombs," my father said. "Your mother will go with you."
And he drives us to the station.

Mum and Betty smoke.
John has gone to war.
Our father's dog-collar saved him, alone now in his Norman church across the narrow road.

I want to be with him,
in the green grass of the church yard, among the humps and dead flowers in jars,
follow his rustling cassock,
smell the bay rum he puts on his hair and feel the sun on my face.

I want to stand in the warm rain that pounds the earth
and splashes up my legs,
reach up into branches heavy with *Beauty of Bath*,
Pick one and smell it,
Sink my teeth into it,
Delicious first fruits
where inside it is
    pink
like dawn through faded curtains.

WORDS-WORTH

Faded roses climb the papered walls.
A voice cuts through the dawn light
And a smell of toast.

One more minute.
One more minute under the blanket.

My feet touch the freezing lino
To stay cold and chilblained all day
Itching under the ink-stained desk.

Stop fidgeting, and read me that last line.
What does it mean?
Everyone stares.
I swallow nothing down the dry gorge of my throat.

Outside the window daffodils nod,
Trumpeting their silent messages.

The voice drones on — I smell the lead in my pencil.
Suddenly I'm washed in a sea of yellow
And, floating above the Eton crops
And pigtails of my classmates,

I drift through the window
Caught on a golden cloud,
Chilblains, nits and the Wordy Bard
Forgotten.

ON THE BEACH
- 1943 -

The grey sea laps the shores of Norfolk.
The muddy geese-strewn marshes are wired off;
Doesn't stop us children plundering
A washed up German ship
And finding a bloated body
In the blasted hold.

SOFT WHITE SLICED

1941

I was twelve when I had my first crush.

He was older than me – nineteen – and drove a baker's van, calling at our house twice a week.

On school holidays I would hover about in the kitchen, watching the tantalisingly slow hands of the big clock on the wall creep round towards his usual delivery time, waiting for the crunch of the tyres on the gravelled drive and the slam of the van door – sounds that invariably caused me to be swept off in an ecstasy of electric thrills and to chew the collar of my blouse. Whenever she felt excited or anxious, my sister Pat bit her nails; I chewed the collar of my blouse. I don't think I had one blouse or dress with a collar that wasn't frayed at the edges.

'You mustn't do that,' admonished my mother, who thought she ought to say something – more out of duty than concern for what I was doing. She would look at me, her soft grey eyes not really cross, but with an expression of 'Do you really have to do that?', as she gave her knitting needles an upward jab to release more wool from the ball in her lap, reluctant to delve too deep lest she find something strange in her middle daughter to cause her concern.

Ella would answer Gordon's knock.

'Morning Gordon.'

'Morning Ella.'

And into the kitchen he would swagger, carrying over his arm a large square basket of still warm loaves, and glance across to where I was pretending to be doing something at the sink.

'Hello Pam, all right?'

I would nod, chewing, taking in his fair curly hair, his sun-tanned face, a white apron tied around his waist, and thinking: he was the most gorgeous thing I had ever seen.

This painfully ecstatic scenario went on for most of the long summer of 1943 till one day, when I was cycling with my friend Amy, she told me about a film she had seen the night before at the local cinema.

'I was in the back row and who should be sitting next to me but Gordon Finn, canoodling with some blond girl. I couldn't get a good look but on the way out they had their arms round each other.'

I felt my bike wobble as I digested this awful news.

2007

I sometimes see Gordon in our local supermarket wrestling with a wayward trolley as his wife pokes around the shelves.

'Hello Pam, all right?', he asks.

I nod and shift my weight onto the stick I use since my hip op.

He has grown bald and paunchy and, if he still wore it, his baker's apron would now need longer tapes. But I can't help noticing, among the lager six-packs in his trolley, instead of those lovely warm loaves, just a wrapped soft white sliced.

DRAUGHTS

Sometimes Gordon's father Bill who owned the bakery in the next village would deliver to us. Always disappointing to me when I saw his large red-faced countenance emerge from the van and come up to the back door whistling, basket over his arm when I had forgotten it was Gordon's day off.

But not so my father who was a keen draughts player and had somehow found out that Bill was too. He had already laid out the board in the sitting room, knowing that Bill couldn't resist a quick game on his rounds and the cup of coffee that Ella would bring him. More often than not, they would get so involved that the housewives from the cottages nearby, knowing where he was, would have to come the Rectory for their bread and Bill had to go out to the van and serve them.

"I see your van go by over an hour ago", Elsie Marsh in her wrap-around pinafore would say, grabbing her loaf from Bill.

"S'alright," says Bill, "I'm just havin' a word with the Rector."

"Hm ... long word, I must say. Wha' about my Bert's dinner? He ha'er go back up the field. And I hen't go' no bread atum."

And she stamps off swearing "Funny bloody baker".

LADY IN GREEN

Lady in Green reflecting summer —
Chagall could have painted her
Flying over her barn, clutching flowers.

I've never seen so many daffodils
That flank her drive in spring
Spreading sundrops on the meadows.
William's pen would have flourished.

Her kitchen smells of herbs —
Gossamer thread-collectors
That catch the evening sun.

We sit by an open window.
A blackbird's dulcet tones claim his pad;
Bees drone in and out —
Opium-ridden ginger-haired thugs
On snarling motorbikes.

The fields turn to gold;
A barn owl flaps its leisurely way
Along the hedge.

I rise quietly, leaving the still moment...
And my Lady in Green.

PIGGY

Piggy died today at noon. He'd had a stroke in the night and I found him lying on the kitchen floor when I came down in the morning. He was still breathing, but his eyes had gone up and I knew he was going.

I called Murray. He came downstairs and phoned the vet. When the vet came, he told me that Piggy wouldn't get over the stroke and he needed to give him a lethal shot to help him on his way. Within minutes Piggy was gone. Murray had to go out so the vet stayed with me until his return. It was a great comfort.

Murray buried Piggy near the trees in the corner of the garden and made a little grave for him. On the wall he wrote "PIGGY".

Piggy died like the gentleman and aristocrat that he was, quietly and with no fuss. I have been unable to stop crying all day.

ELLY

The damp fields squelch.
I look for you
To come bounding.
But there's only the peewit
And a dark shadow,
A watery sun
And geese embroidering
The silence of the late afternoon.
Twigs creak in the wind.
I stand near the hedge.
A rustle. Is it you?

Fourteen years!
Was that old?
Must be.
Routine was comfort.
We knew things, you and I.
But at the end you didn't
When he came with the syringe
And your pain was gone.

He took you away
Leaving silence
And space,
Torpor around the house,
And the empty,
Dripping garden.

STREAM

A little rushing sound:
Baby of the mountains.
Stars of sunlight glint in the ripple
Where a wagtail bobs on a stone
And then skims upstream —
A yellow dart —
Away into the pied world of low willows,
Their green hair streaming in the rill:
Ophelia's grave.

Molly lumbers over
And breathes her sweet grassy breath on my
  neck.
I smell her familiar milky cowness
As she looks at me with bovine curiosity
Under lashes that glossy page girls would die for.

As I look back at her, mists swirling in my head,
I know that my salty tears will one day reach the
  sea.

NOVEMBER GARDEN

Trees wave spiky arms.
A blackbird sways on a twig
And flies off chortling,
Leaving droplets of bright water
Falling on brown rose heads,
The pink scented beauty of their June glory
Filling my nostrils as I scuff
Through the once green garb of summer.

WHITEOUT

God is plucking his snow goose!
Feathers swirl about
As in a glass ball at Christmas.

I stand on the lawn,
Arms outstretched —
Gormley's Angel.
I will freeze into that shape:
A forever crucifix
Where rows of swallows gather in September.

From his stable, Trojan looks at me
Across the whitening yard.
He mutters a throaty greeting;
I kiss his velvet nose;
He tosses his head
And clicks his heals,
Arrogant as a Spanish dancer.
'Soon,' I say, 'soon we will gallop.'

Crunching across the virgin fields with Ben,
His Labrador footprints
Strangely lupine in the snow,
I leave the house behind
Standing like an iced cake on its doily
And shout into the blur
'God, can you hear me
Through all those feathers?'
There is no booming reply
Through the blizzard,
Just a whish of snowflakes
Falling on the silent fields
And melting on my eyelashes.

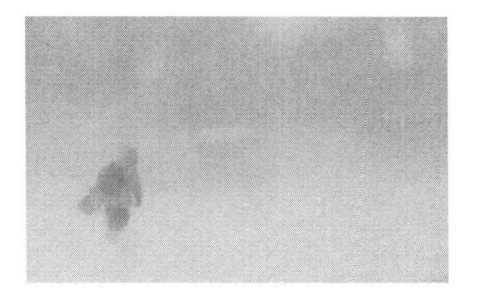

NOVEMBER WALK

Chinese Emperors* crowned with gold
Stand, as the last bastions of summer,
In their ranks along the hedgerows
Ablaze with bird-ripe berries.

Blond grasses sway in the wind,
Blowing kisses to the spring.

A family of long-tailed tits accompanies me
As they flit from twig to twig,
Their tiny wild sounds awakening
A Lazarus of dreams.

* Hogweed

WINDY SHORE

Cavernous mouth sucks
Only to throw up again
Like an orca whale playing with a seal;
Stones sting my legs
And salt leaves a white rim on my dress.

Cold and blue and crashing:
Ego disappears.
A sort of death occurs to mundanity,
And I am swept clean
By the besom of the shore.

Across the waves the knights are riding,
Their shining armour glistens in the sun.
And on the shore white sand spirals –
Sandcastles of the wind.

THE SEA

Aphrodite, Neptune's Miss,
Flirtatious – blue – fecund,
Her heaving white-laced bosom
Belies the secrets of her womb.

TIDE TURN

White lips lick the sand,
Devouring, lapping,
Filling little channels
And dribbling into footprints.
People move up to the dunes
Calling their kids.
Gulls start to screech,
Borne on warm spirals,
White quarrelsome creatures
Diving for shrimps.
We play the shore game
Running down at the suck,
Judging the frozen moment
Before the huge wave breaks.
A sense of urgency fills the beach,
Sails are hauled and voices call out
'Get in', 'Man the tiller', 'Board down'
And a flurry of red, white and blue
Tacks off on a perfect force 4:
Computer whizz-kids, prized from their seats,
Are out to play.

EGGSHELLS

I don't like walking on eggshells:
It seems the place is full of them
Crunching under my heavy tread.

If only I could walk lightly.
But they would still be crushed
Into nothingness …
… or powder at best.

Perhaps I should stay on the pathways.
But then I'd never learn
To tread more carefully,
To pick my way, perhaps.

But then, aren't eggshells good for the earth?
Grit, and all that …?

ROUNDED

I like a rounded world.
It feels safe.
I can't fall off.

I like all round things —
Peaches, my baby's cheeks, balls;
Dartboards and balloons,
Rounding up the horses ...
... and my kids.

Tea-time: round cakes.

SWEET PEAS

Pink, apricot, violet, white,
Translucent fans of sheer delight,
I've got them on my window sill
Where they will bloom today until
They droop and lose their gorgeous scent;
But more will come where they just went.

BLABBERRY

She comes in
We chat
Both want to relate recent happenings
The words tumble
Bubble out
Our minds wobble
Confused.
What?
Oh yes, I see.
But I don't see
Or understand
Because there's no time to digest.
I've got violent indigestion
Stop.
I'll just go to the loo
Back in a minute —
Necessary break
In the east/west storm of blabbery.
But I love her to bits.
I need to spend a day with her
Or a year —
Time to spread it out a bit.
It's the same on the phone.
I usually put the receiver down, sweating.
I want to enjoy what she's telling me
And not butt in with all my own doings.
We are verbally falling over each other.
Bugger.

NEXT TIME, BIRO

Are you feeling more obliging today
Because I'm in the mood to write.
Yes? Ok, let's go then.
...
Another winter approaches
With dark afternoons
And long evenings.

What do we do?
Watch the box?
Phone people who don't want to talk?
They are in the middle of their soaps
Or getting supper — or eating it
Or putting the kids to bed
Or having a row — or in the bath.

Oh God, it's only 7 o'clock.
A bit early for Horlicks — or a nightcap.

So, Pen, I'll just keep scribbling
To see what comes out.
Not much yet, I notice.
You can do better than that.
Next time ... Next time?

Actually I've just thought of something:

Nothing ever dies because of the *modus operandi* of the genius.

And then:
Why do women carry those huge shoulder bags that stick out at the back, knocking everybody over?

SHARP FINS

Bags that stick out like giant fins
On the shoulders of shoppers
Could turn any minute and knock me sideways.

And rucksacks on the backs of jolly hikers,
Huge monstrosities that expand a person
Into a massive hunchback.

I shrink against the shelves
As they heave by, turning this way and that.

And yes, here it comes –
The sharp fin of a bag lady.

I dive past it to the check-out,
Thanking God for plastic bags ...
Recyclable, of course.

GREEDY PIG

I'm fat:
I don't know when I've had enough.

Greedy Pig,
Scoffing all the chocolates.

Is it because I came from a large family
And the box was always empty
Unless I got there first?

We were all skinny then
During the war:
Ration books everywhere,
Living on potato soup,
Standing in long queues,
Pulling at my mother's coat –
Hungry.

Maybe that's what's wrong with me.

HURRAY

The bathwater covers my stomach
And I can get out of the bath.

I can do up my skirts
And see my ankle bones again.

I can turn over in bed
And walk more than three yards without puffing.

I can hug my children without a mountain between us
And wear fitted dresses …
                     … With a belt!

I can get out of the car.

      AND I CAN EAT A PIECE OF CHOCOLATE!

The V in front of my jeans has closed
And my knees look less like oak-trees.

I no longer rush to hide in the loo
When the cameras come out.

How did I do it?

      BY JOINING **WEIGHT-WATCHERS**

             EASY PEASY

           DO IT TODAY

COW

I want to make
A cow.
I think I'll do it
In clay.
It doesn't work
With paint.

Why don't I
Buy a cow
And keep it in the garden
And milk it twice a day?

I could make
Cheese and butter
And not run out of milk.

My friends would be
Impressed
To see my huge new pet
Lumbering about
The rose-beds
And staring through the door.

It would be like a dog …
And lots of manure, too.

Perhaps I could train it
To shit on the compost heap.

Wow! I could be on Look East for that.

Oil paint doesn't smell of cows.
It isn't warm and snotty.
It doesn't look at me with soft brown eyes
And always gets the legs wrong.

SNOWDROPS

We spread our white skirts to the pale morning, showing the frilly petticoats edged with green lace that we have been making all winter.

We are the brides of spring, pure and white.

We lift our heads to our flaky cousins who kiss us softly and are gone in a whisper.

We are sometimes picked and put into glass jars and placed on windowsills where we command the scene. All else fades into nothingness in our presence.

Our wild earthy scent makes you pull at your chains.

RECYCLING

White aprons,
> Newly washed,

Bulge over green dresses.

The fat ladies of spring* are strutting their stuff
> Along the hedgerows.

Their scent is enormous,
> Biting my nostrils with sweet reassurance.

The stench of rotting leaves forgotten.
> Kill?
>> Shout?
>>> Stab?

You can't get me,
> I'm on my bike.

* Blackthorn

FIONA

Long skirts, beads, big hair, dope and Beatle-mania. Stepping over comatose bodies at muddy raves, Murray and I were in our thirties in the sixties, 'grooving it' a bit, too, although it was difficult with two young kids in tow.

I had this friend, Fiona. Fin we called her. She, too, was married with two kids. We used to meet at weekends and do things together, like going to the beach, or getting Grannies to have the kids so we could spend nights in the pub.

At the time this partying was going on, Fin took up with a bloke she'd met at Glastonbury. With bracelets jangling and tossing her long flaxen hair, the musk scent she used stinging our nostrils, she declared one day that she was crazy about him and that they were going to run away together.

We stared at her. Was this a joke? Or was she really about to leave her family to live in a commune just to get into the sack with a guitar-twanging, long black-haired hippy sporting a studded leather jacket, jeans with the knees out, rings hanging from every protrusion (the ones you could see), and a walrus moustache?

And yes, she was. She was away for three or four months, none of us hearing a word from her while her husband Tim stayed at home juggling work and kids.

One day she walked in on them while Tim was getting the tea ready and told him that the bloke she was with had 'moved on' with some 'groovy chick' to another place. Could she come home?

"No," he said. "I want a divorce."

So they split up, living separately and sharing the kids.

Fin was still coming round to our house, flinging herself about and sighing, hair and long skirts draped over the sofa, smoking dope and making googoo eyes at Murray.

"Fin," I said, "you can stop that at once. I know you want to find yourself a man, but it ain't gonna be here!"

I didn't see her much after that.

BLOOD

She bled to death:
She was anaemic.
She died of leukaemia:
She had no blood.

I was pale and thin —
Was I going to die too?
I lost blood in haemorrhages,
in cuts and accidents and operations.

I am afraid of blood:
I don't like seeing it.
Even menstruation scared me.

I lost a river of blood
when my hymen was broken.
Sex, blood, Christ, sacrament.

If you loose all your blood, you die —
You've got to keep your blood:
You mustn't bleed.
How dare you take my blood?

Go away with your beastly needle.

SEPTEMBER WALK

Corn marigolds flame bright
As suns around the edges of the stubble,

    And, with black fruit bulging
    From the hedgerows,

        What more do I want
        On a fine

            September afternoon?

ON FINDING A GIRL'S BODY IN A WOOD

Pale morning, March winds are catching in her hair:
    Some men are there attending to it all.
I call my dog, we're not to go in there.

It's early yet, but she was unaware
Of stealth and beastliness that stalked her through
    the night she danced away without a care.

The swaying branches wait for when their time has come to bear
    Green buds of May, to blossom forth fecund,
Their principle of life exuberantly clear.

Not so the one that's been chopped down,
    Her scarlet nails and white dress smirched
With sodden leaves that pad the woodland floor
    Where Artemis once danced – but now no more.

EMERGENCE

I sit in my white bed enveloped by pillows like the early summer clouds that pass over the garden.

In the flowerbeds huge oriental poppy buds, pregnant with scarlet booty, await their cue to burst into a flamenco of Spanish skirts.

I look at my new great-grandson Dylan. His name means 'Old Man of the Sea' — like his great-grandfather who sits on my bed holding him tenderly.

I get up quietly, leaving them in their white ship to sail the seven seas.

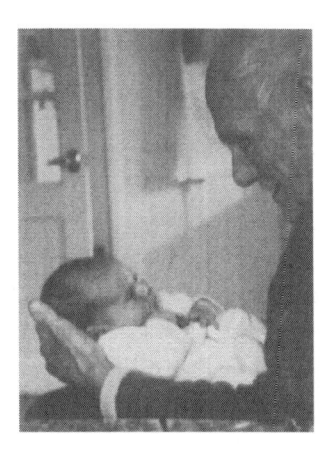

THE STREAM

There was once a woman who found it difficult to reach decisions. She would dither about this way and that, her mind in a turmoil of thoughts, torn between the conflicting choices that presented themselves, her heart heavy and lost.

This inability to decide made her terribly unhappy.

One day she had a big decision to take. Not knowing what to do, she went for a long walk in the country, hoping to clear her head. Walking in the country was not something she normally did. She packed a little bag with food and water and set off, passing fields and cottage gardens and children playing in sandy lanes.

After an hour she came to a mossy bank among some trees by a stream.

She sat down on the soft ground and ate her bread and drank her water, dangling her weary feet in the cool flowing stream. She began to feel drowsy and lay down on the mossy bank, listening to the murmur of the gurgling water and enjoying the caress of the soft summer air upon her face. Presently she fell asleep.

As she slept she had a dream. She dreamt the stream was talking to her, telling her of its life that had begun in a spring high up in the hills and how it had wound its way round all sorts of obstacles to find its level which was the only course it could take. It couldn't jump over rocks and boulders: it had to flow round them.

As it continued whispering to her, the woman began to feel at one with the stream. She felt the cool of the ripples and the steady flow all around and through her, and a great calm came over her as she sensed herself being swept gently along by the purposeful flow with only one thing in mind: to reach the sea.

After a long and beautiful journey, the woman tasted salt on her lips. She knew she had reached the sea and knew now, too, which way she must decide.

When at last the trees surrounding the river shimmered and stirred in the late afternoon breeze, she awoke and stretched her arms and legs. She was more relaxed and content than she had felt for a long time, overwhelmed by an intense gratitude to the stream for the message it had given her and the knowledge that she would be able to relive what she had experienced at any time. She rose, packed her bag and set off back the way she came.

Once home, she settled down, her feet up on the sofa with a cup of tea warming her hands. She reached for the knitting she had abandoned over the past few days, excited now to see the tiny white jacket take shape.

~~~~

I am grateful to that stream: I now have the most beautiful granddaughter.

A GRANDMOTHER'S STORY

Anxiety looks out from the pale quiet face. Defeated, trapped, my girl is in a turmoil of emotions: first longing, then panic, then longing again, gripped by a myriad of complex moods and lost.

I know by your face, my darling: there is no need for words. I panic for a day, a week, as the months creep by towards the inevitable time. And when at last it comes, I fall in love with what I see: brand new, alive, straight eyebrows, dark and beautiful. She stays by me and I learn to love again: the tiny form that grows and talks and laughs. I laugh with her all down the mixed-up years, my sadness at the absence of a father like my own touching me as I love and weep with her.

And now she's grown eighteen and gone away.

I miss her happy wisdom, and our silly times together.

And the things we learned, discussed and made, are still in my drawer with their edges curling up.

THE LANE

On a late afternoon in November I sit on an elm stump
and remember the giant trees
that once flanked this path with its snake of green
winding up the middle.

The gypsies used to come and park their vardos
on the greensward, letting their black-eyed children play,
guarded by a lurcher tied to a wheel.

They would give me tea in a Crown Derby cup
and stir it with a golden spoon.
Elsa told my fortune once,
reading my twelve year-old palm.
'You'll marry a sailor,' she said. And of course I did.

What am I doing up here – silly old fool,
groggy on my pins and leaning on a stick?
But I can't *not* come:
I have to have my fix of the melancholy silence –
broken only by the distant mew of a pewit
from across the brown fields.

And, as the hunter's moon appears
and the earth tilts towards the night,
I know my sojourn is complete.

I can go home now –
perhaps until the summer when the gypsies might be here.

MY SAILOR

I once had a crush on a boy
But he threw me away like a toy;
When he found someone else,
I was left on the shelf.
But I soon found a sailor, ahoy.

My sailor, he taught me to sail:
We went bounding all over the main.
With him at the helm and me at the bail,
I was happy, oh happy, again.

And that wasn't all, let me say:
We got wed on a beautiful day.
In April it was, in the spring
With lilacs and birds on the wing.

We've still got a boat on the lawn
A bit batter'd now, with its sails all torn.
She misses the sea and, yes, so do we,
But we've done now with rounding the Horn.

NIGHT SAIL

I move the tiller
Catch another wind
Sails bloat
We surge forward
Power in my belly
Bumping the furrows
White lip snarling on the bow
Gulls scream overhead
I am alive
One wrong move and I'm in the drink

Turning over
Stiff in my bones and holding the sheet
I lick the salt off my lips

ZIMMER FRAME

Why it's called a 'Zimmer' frame
I've no idea.
It's nothing like a 'Zimmer'.
The very word zimms.
I can't imagine this thing 'zimming' —
Its magneted 100% to the ground,
Only lifting an inch
To go forward,
Clung onto by hands
That once clung to ski poles
And tillers.

Feet clad in old moccasins
That once wore ski boots
Or deck shoes
That gripped the long boards
Or heaving decks.
Shuffle, shuffle, shuffle.
I can hear him shambling
Down the corridor
Until his bent frame
Slumps into a chair.

If this is old age
I'm ★ ★ ★ ★ ED if I want it.

OLD SAILOR

I hesitate outside his door.
Is he asleep?
I wonder if he wants a drink
Or a hug.
His eyes are closed, the woolly hat
Askew.

The duvet rises up and down,
Another day.

I walk towards the bed and then
His eyes slit open:
Small pools left by ebbing tides.

UNRAVELLING

Staggering
Hunched
Heading for his bed
Where he will lie for most of the day
His crucified hands picking
    at the stitches of his blanket.

FROZEN

What can I do but stay apart
        in the North wing
since you gave up the ghost and took to your bed,
        frozen with fear
              of falling,
                    of dying,
                            of your face in the mirror?

I walk to the South rooms
        where you sit in a wheeled chair,
              like the pram you remember
being gently pushed by your mother's loving hands
        and seeing her smiling face
              forever from your pillow.

        But I am no longer her now;
        and so I pass the buck:
    withdraw from the aura of a need so great
        that it freezes the bones
            of my octogenarian stoop.

MIRROR IMAGE

I used to look at my Granny whenever she stayed with us, wrinkled and old, arthritic and waving her stick. She came more often after Grandpa died, for weeks on end it seemed, driving us all mad, especially my mother who couldn't really say much. She just put up with it, while my father stayed in his study for most of the day.

My sisters and I escaped on our bikes down to Blakeney to swim in the channel and watch the boats coming in on the tide, filled with cockles and leather-faced fishermen — we knew them all and would stand in the rising water, waving at them, our knitted swimsuits hanging down, thin brown wartime children who ate raw turnips from the fields and made dampers from flour and water.

My Granny didn't come one summer. "She's ill", my mother said, and went down south to see her. She cried when she came home.

But grannies don't give up so easily. They tend to hang around ... until one day, they sneak back in to hide behind the mirror.

INSOMNIA

Awake all night, wearing out the sheets,
Bung-eyed and cross in the morning.
When will I catch up?
I will die without sleep!
Take a pill?
No, I feel ghastly on pills.
I've got a 'thing' about them:
If I take one, I lie there rigid
Wondering what it's going to do to me.
Will I go mad? Or explode?

Get up and make a cuppa?
Might as well fill up with caffeine and really get going.
Not a bad idea,
And a run round the garden, perhaps.
Except that it would excite the dog
Who might get geared up for a moonlight walk
And begin to bark.
That would rouse HIM and he would dodder out,
Bleary-eyed and riddled with pills.
WOS going on? OOZAT?
As he grabs the oar he keeps at the front door.

I creep back into my room, taking the dog
Who farts all night.
I sprinkle lavender to no avail.

At last the clock says six, so I stagger into the kitchen,
Make a cuppa tea and take it back to bed.
The pigeons in the ash tree moan their dirge
"My toe hurts, Betty".

DIAMOND

They come, some on sticks,
Up the path – is that really her?
(he's long gone, of course).
The old familiar laughter is in her eyes
As I greet her at the door.
"Come in," I say, hugging her.
She smells lovely: faint flowers –
Must be the soap she uses –
She never was one for scent.
"How are you, May?
I haven't seen you for ages.
It's only on these occasions
That we ever meet!
I wish we lived nearer, like we used to."
Her white curls nod,
Done for the party.

They gather round: beloved faces,
And raise their flutes to Murray and me.

MAY

Through stained glass a soft light colours the side of her
    last coat;
and on her head a half-moon of wild flowers shimmers.
               No half-moon about her, I think
               Sitting in my black.
               She circled the earth
               Wisely and fully
               For ninety-three years in all,
               Her long plait over her shoulder
               Or wound around her head,
               As she fed her turkeys
               and made jam from plump Victorias.
She lies now, quiet to the *'Bright and Beautiful'* chorus we
    sing to her.
"Thank you," she says and, practical as ever, "I am just
    getting on with another job".
A kaleidoscope of colour dances with the trees and falls
               like petals on our heads
                       as the brief hour passes.

SHUTTERINGS

Summer days in the garden:
I sit by the hollyhocks and roses.
Shadows move as the sun
Swings across the day.
I don't need a clock:
When that shadow falls
Upon that patch of grass,
I know it's time to get the lunch
For him and me.

One each side of the peeling table,
We eat our salad
And our strawberries.
He falls asleep.
I lean back
In my chair
And dust off the old box brownie,
My eyelids shuttering through pictures
black and white:

Parents and siblings appear
All gone now bar one:
Harvest time in the fields,
The pungent smell of horse sweat;
I ride side-saddle on Prince,
My thin legs dangling,
My hand holding the tees
On the huge horse collar;
Christmas parties in people's houses,
Wearing homemade dresses —

Awful things — all the same
Like children from an orphanage.
My father appears,
The black skirts of his cassock
Blowing round his ankles.
I follow him through the churchyard
Into the dark interior and musty smell
Of the little Norman church
Where he will prepare
His morning service.
I help him clear the bats' droppings
That have hailed
On every pew and prayer book.
He opens the Bible on the lectern
Shaped like a bird of prey with outstretched wings
And finds the Lesson for the Day
Which old Colonel Simpkin Jones
Will mumble through inaudibly
And during which my sisters and I will play
Happy Families
In the front pew low down
So it looks as if we're praying.
Which pleases our father no end.
My mother next to us
Sits in her pert hat looking blank
And trying not to notice too much.

I shift in the uncomfortable canvas chair.
A soft wind ruffles
The leaves of the acacia tree
And my hair.
I glance at Murray — his mouth is open.
I just hope a fly doesn't go into it.

UNKNOWING *

The room darkens
Around the green chair
Where I sit.

The dog snores
Curled up on her bed:
A black blob.

The garden door
Swinging in the night wind
Thuds softly.

And in the gaps
A sickle moon appears
And disappears.

Elusive as a fly
Tomorrow's horizon fades
Into *ultima Thule*.

* As Murray lies in hospital

WINDOWS OF SUMMER

New green out there
Through double glazing now,
Not through the thin glass and wood
That rattled on windy nights ...
Strangely comforting.

Squares of time
Move like molten glass
In sun-drenched frames:
The putty has shrunk and cracked.
Bits fall off
Broken panes, letting in the birds.

Apple trees nudge the brick,
Lichen covered and bent,
Their wizened crop falling,
Nourishing the earth.

Secret places: where butterflies dance
And birds nest undisturbed,
Elderflowers spread their scented plates
In the new green out there
Through the windows of summer.

ROSE
To my dying Mother

It stands in a jar,
Pink as a baby's cheek
Scenting the room
And my dreams.

Your sweet face looks out at me
From the silver-framed window,
A labyrinth of velvet years
And attar of roses.

* * *

We stood by the gate;
You snipped one off
And said
"Drive carefully, darling".

DAYS

No hour,
No clock,
Only dandelions and the sun.

Funny old woman
Stained by the past
But somehow glad of the whole business.

Glad of the absence
Of velvet cushions
And strawberries and cream.

CHRISTMAS

Tinsel and wine and flushed faces —
All very well for a time.
But let me out for a moment:
I need to cool off
away from the pulsating house
where my middle-aged children
and their children
and their children
Congregate and scream and suck bottles,
pour each other G and Ts
and laugh.

I love them with my heart,
Especially the tiny new one
born of my darling.
But just for five minutes, please,
I must go for a little way
into the silence of the night
and feel the east wind
biting through my coat,
and see the sickle moon
cold and high.

Time to go back, I think.
They'll be wondering where I am.
I call the dog
snuffling in the wood
and turn towards my home
where they have all come
to be with me.

WHAT ARE WE?

What are we?
Scrabblers
Like wild boars
After truffles.

Techno aside,
The primal urge
To keep warm, eat and mate
Is all – let's go for it.

From Queen to Masai Warrior
With his cows and blood and milk,
And the wandering dreamtime Abbo,
We are herd animals
Running with the wolves of time:
Migrating wildebeests
Pounced on by lions,
Ripped to pieces and devoured.

There, but for the Grace of God, ...

TIME BOMB

Black and white:
I see it every morning
        And in the evening;
Lift it up when I dust my dressing table,
Silver framed, small, precious
        Two faces.

Where are you?
Your hand is on her shoulder.
She stands smiling for the snap
        Wearing a jumper
        She had spent the winter knitting.

I sit on my bed – staring
        Unbelieving for a moment.
Did it really happen?
Enemy planes droning overhead
Laden with bombs?
Sirens wailing
And a scuttle to the underground shelter
Across the snowy garden,
Freezing and terrified like cornered rats?

Roses blooming in lush summer borders
Among the oriental poppies and delphiniums?
Cups of tea on the lawn,
        My mother smoking a cigarette
        And Father in the customary linen
            jacket that he wore in summer?

How have I ever existed,
eaten,
    drunk,
        bathed,
            spoken,
been a wife,
    brought up my children,
        loved, hated,
            worked,
laughed, cried –
                since?

I look in the mirror over your frozen heads:
I am older than you now.

CUCKOO

Alert I stand and gape in awe;
My ears are strained to burst.

Why is it so important
That I should hear it first?

MY BLOKE

Old man
Young once
My bloke

BABY SITTING

Two years old.
She stands, legs apart:
A picture of chunky defiance, testing her mother.

I cringe in the corner, ears exploding.

But then, after the bath, warm and cuddly.
She sits on my lap in pyjamas dotted with pink teddy
    bears.

I smell her washed hair
as her fat little hands scrabble the pages of a picture
    book.

She stretches and yawns.

I carry her to her cot and settle her down,
creep out of the door
and down to where my daughter is putting on her coat.

"Shan't be long, Mum", as she goes off to meet Tom.

I flop down with a G&T and a bit of tat on the box,
always with an ear for the threatening-looking object
    on the coffee table.

THE DANCE

I lift her up,
        My hands strong under her armpits.
A warm and woolly bundle,
        Plump and cuddly,
Her soft breath upon my neck.

She knows me now and is content
To let me hold her close and sweet,
        Smelling of powder.
She looks at me with china blue eyes,
Whose depths I cannot fathom.

I love her with my heart,
        This tiny newish thing.
She moves to a primal rhythm in my arms,
        Ra Ra Ra, she sings,
Her starfish fingers spread,

And we dance.

PORTRAIT

He had it painted of me from a photograph
At two years old in cream silk dress with smocking.
I see in me my two-year old great granddaughter:
Which means I shall live on.

Perhaps she'll wander in wild places
As I did long ago —
And, in my head, still do
As the rays of sunshine slide across my bed
And in my afternoon siesta,
       I dream,
              and smell
The almond-scented gorse,
            and feel
The linnet's nest
       hand-warmed by eggs inside;

Play with my sisters and the village kids
Among the ruins, as cows chew cud and stare
And ivy stalks grow thick towards the sky;
Pick bullaces and gorge ourselves until we're sick.
It's wartime: not much food about.

NOVEMBER CHORUS
Wild Geese

A swathe of vermilion silk,
embroidered with black feather-stitch
backs the tuning of a thousand dulcet tones.

I stand in the pit and wait until the orchestra
reaches a Wagnerian crescendo.

Stones move,
grasses wave
and my wings open.

As the sound fades and the silk curtain falls,
a huge orange moon starts to rise above the sea.

SAFFRON MOON

Saffron Moon

Veiled in mist

Still as death